Object ~~Lessons~~
That Teach Bible Truths

Object Lessons That Teach Bible Truths

William C. Hendricks

and

Merle Den Bleyker

BAKER BOOK HOUSE

Grand Rapids, Michigan

First printing, July 1978
Second printing, June 1979
Third printing, April 1981
Fourth printing, February 1983
Fifth printing, July 1984
Sixth printing, December 1985
Seventh printing, April 1987

Contents

1   Baptism

Object: A license plate of a car
Concept: Baptism shows others that we belong to God.
Text: *I Corinthians 12:13* "For by one Spirit we were all baptized into one body. . . ."

Boys and girls, I'm sure that you recognize this object I am holding in my hand *(hold up the license plate)*. Your car has license plates with letters and numbers. Every set of license plates has different numbers and letters.

First, do you see this name here on the plate? *(Point to the name of the state and read it aloud.)* This is the name of the state in which we live. Every car, truck, and school bus in our state has a license plate with the name of our state on it.

Now let's look at the numbers and letters. Who can read the numbers and letters on this license plate? *(Hold the plate up and allow a child to read the numbers and letters aloud.)* If two cars are the same color, and look alike, we might not be able to tell which one belongs to us. But we can easily tell them apart by the license plates. The numbers and letters on my license plate are different from the numbers and letters on your license plate.

If your car was lost or stolen, the police would look for it. But the police might have a hard time knowing which car was your car unless they knew what was on your license plates. By reading the numbers and letters on the license plates, the police could tell if the car they found belongs to you.

Baptism is something like the license plate on your car *(hold up the plate again)*. This license plate says that the car belongs to me. When you are baptized with this water, you are showing people that you belong to Jesus. Baptism is an outward sign to other people that you have been washed clean by Jesus' blood and therefore you belong to Him.

But being baptized isn't *exactly* like a license plate. We can always see the license plates on a car. But after we are baptized, we can't see anything different. The water dries up and disappears. And we certainly don't carry license plates around our necks, do we? Baptism is just one part of belonging to Jesus. God wants us to do the things that please Him every day, so that other people will always be able to see that we belong to Him.

2 Christian

Object: A hot dog and bun with ketchup and mustard
Concept: A Christian has Christ in his heart.
Text: *Galatians 2:20* "I have been crucified with Christ; it is no longer I who live, but Christ who lives in me. . . ."

Who here likes hot dogs? *(Hold up your hand and wait to see if anyone else raises his hand.)* Almost everybody does! But I once read about someone who really loved hot dogs. His name was Mike Wright, and he lives in England. In December 1971 he ate eighteen hot dogs in five minutes!

Some people like ketchup on their hot dogs. Others want ketchup and mustard. Maybe you even like to have some onions and pickle relish on your hot dog. Now, let's look at this hot dog very carefully. What do we have here? What makes this a hot dog? *(Let the children give their answers.)*

If I take the hot dog out of the bun and just eat the ketchup and the mustard, do you think that I am eating a hot dog? *(Hide the hot dog meat from view and hold up only the remaining bun.)* Of course not! A hot dog isn't a hot dog if it doesn't have the meat.

Did you know that a Christian is like a hot dog? A Christian is someone who loves Jesus and wants to do what pleases Him. Just as a hot dog isn't a hog dog without the meat, a person isn't a Christian

9

without Christ. The Bible says that Christ lives in our hearts when we love Him.

In the Book of Acts we read a story about some people who pretended to be Christians but Christ didn't live in their hearts. Their names were Ananias and Sapphira. They sold some of their land and brought the money to Peter. They told Peter that they were giving all of the money to God. But they really kept some of the money at home. They wanted the other Christians to think that they were generous and good Christians. God told Peter that Ananias and Sapphira were lying. They weren't Christians because Christ didn't live in their hearts.

We can't be Christians if we don't have Christ in our hearts. That's just like a hot dog can't be a hot dog without the meat. When Christ lives in our hearts He will help us to live like we should, like Christians.

When you eat a hot dog at your next picnic, let the hot dog remind you that it is only possible to be a Christian if you let Christ live inside your hearts.

3 Church Membership

Object: Trademarks

Concept: A church member wears the trademark of Christ for everyone to see.

Text: *I Corinthians 12:27* "Now you are the body of Christ and indi-
vidually members of it."

Boys and girls, have you ever seen a trademark? A trademark is a
special seal or a small design of a company name. I have a few examples
here with me. *(Hold up your pen.)* This is my pen and if you look at
the clip carefully, you can read the name. *(Read—Eversharp, Parker, or
whatever the name may be.)* That tells what company made this pen.
Or I can look at my watch *(do so)* and written right on the face where
anyone can see it is the maker's name *(read the name on your watch)*. I
can even look inside of my coat *(hold your coat open to show the label
on the inside pocket)* and right there is a label that tells what company
made it.

If this was a poor pen or if my watch wouldn't keep time well, or if
my coat came loose at the seams, I guess the company whose name was
so plainly written on it would be quite ashamed. So before a company
will put its name or trademark on the product it sells, it does its best to
make sure the product is a good one.

Each of you boys and girls is in church this morning. Your friends and neighbors know you go to church. It's like having a trademark or a label on you. You are marked as a Christian, a church member.

Because you have that label, people are going to look at you carefully. They will expect you to talk like a Christian and act like a Christian. If they know you go to church on Sunday, they are going to watch to see how you live on Monday and Tuesday and the rest of the week.

But even more important than having your friends and neighbors watching you is the fact that God watches you too. The companies that made my pen and my watch and my coat want their products to do well so that they can be proud of them. So God is pleased if we show our Christian trademarks in everything we do. The church is God's kingdom on earth. As members of the church, we want our lives to glorify God our Maker. We must let our trademarks show!

4 Covenant

Object: A bag of candy (one piece for each child)

Concept: God has made an agreement or covenant with us which He will never forget.

Text: *Genesis 17:7* "And I will establish my covenant between me and you and your descendants after you throughout their generations for an everlasting covenant, to be a God to you and to your descendants after you."

I know that all children love candy. Grownups like it too. This morning I have a big bag of candy *(hold it up for all to see)*. If I wanted to keep this candy for myself, I wouldn't be very kind, would I?

But I'm going to make an agreement with you. Listen very carefully to what I'm going to say. If you do exactly what I say, then we may all have a piece of candy. Do you think that sounds fair? *(Let the children respond.)*

This is the agreement: I promise to give you each a piece of candy. But in order to get a piece you must shake the hand of the boy or girl next to you. That should be easy, so find someone near to you and shake his or her hand *(the children shake hands)*. Very good! You obeyed me perfectly and kept your part of the agreement.

God also made an agreement with us. It's recorded in the Bible. He didn't use candy—He loves us so much that He made an even better promise to us. He said that He would be our God and special friend always if we listen to Him and obey Him.

For your part of the agreement we made together, you shook hands as I asked you to do. For our part of the agreement with God He wants us to listen to Him and obey Him always. A covenant is another name for this kind of agreement.

In God's covenant with us He promises to be our God and we are to serve and obey Him. Since God always keeps His promises, we must do all we can to keep our part of the agreement too.

God keeps His part of the agreement always and since I made a promise as part of our agreement a few minutes ago, I also must keep mine. Here is your candy. You get it because you did what you were supposed to do as your part of the agreement. *(Pass the candy out to the children.)* Let's always remember God's covenant.

5 Covet

Object: An open cardboard box with a hole cut in its side just large enough for your open hand to fit through but small enough that you can't get it out again when you make a fist around the orange or apple inside

Concept: We must not covet or love things so much that we won't let go of them. Loving God must hold first place in our lives.

Text: Matthew 16:26 "For what will it profit a man, if he gains the whole world and forfeits his life?"

One African tribe has a special way of catching monkeys. They make a hole in a gourd just large enough for a monkey to put his paw inside. Then the natives fill the gourd with some nuts or fruit that monkeys like and fasten the gourd tightly to a low branch of a tree.

During the night a monkey comes and reaches through the hole in the gourd. Just imagine that the hole in this box is like the hole in the gourd. *(Show the audience the hole in the side of the box and the apple or orange inside. You may wish to cover the top of the box with some type of cellophane or clear plastic to make the trap seem more real.)*

When the monkey has his hand inside, he grabs a fistful of nuts or fruit like this *(turn the box sideways so the audience can see you grab the orange or apple in your hand and make a fist.)* But when the monkey is ready to run away with the food there is just one problem.

He can't get his hand back out of the monkey trap. *(Demonstrate the monkey's problem by trying to get your closed fist out of the box.)* If the monkey would only open his fist, he could easily get away. *(Let go of the fruit and pull your open hand out of the box.)* But then the monkey would lose his nuts or fruit that he wants so bad. He won't open his hand. Instead, he tires himself out trying all night to get his closed fist out of the monkey trap and in the morning, he is quickly captured.

Sometimes, boys and girls, we act like a monkey in a monkey trap like this. We covet things, that is, we want things. We crave for and desire things so badly even though we can't have them or even though they don't belong to us. We reach out and try to get hold of them and if we do get them, we won't let go.

Jesus said, "What will it profit a man, if he gains the whole world and forfeits his own life?"

Don't get caught in a monkey trap.

6   Creation

Object: An armful of children's winter coats
Concept: God has made the world and all things in it.
Text: *Psalm 104:24* "O Lord, how manifold are thy works! In wisdom hast thou made them all; the earth is full of thy creatures."

It's rather chilly today, isn't it? This morning the radio said that it was going to be cold all day. In fact, it is only about_____degrees. I wore my coat to church so I wouldn't get cold. I'm sure that you did too. Your parents wouldn't want you to go outside without a coat or jacket. How many of you wore your coat to church this morning? Raise your hand if you wore a warm coat like one of these. *(Hold the armful of coats up for all to see and then count the hands.)* Very good! We all came to church warmly dressed.

We are glad for our coats because they protect us from the rain and snow. All of our coats had to be made for us by somebody. Some of us have mothers who can make our coats and some of us have coats that were made by people in a coat factory.

But where does a dog or cat get its fur coat? Did somebody make it for the animals to wear? *(Allow some time for a response.)* No, animals were born with their fur. They have coats to wear all the time. These animals never get very cold because God made coats for them and gave them their fur.

17

People can make pretty things like these coats to keep us warm. But really it's only because of God's wonderful plan of creation that we have a way to get the cloth and the thread to make coats and hats with. He provided these things for us. God also provided for the animals to have the fur coats they need. God is the great creator who planned it all! He made the sun and the stars. He made_____ *(name some local natural feature like a river, mountain or lake).* But best of all, He created you and me. God is a powerful and wise God; He is a wonderful creator.

People can make coats like these *(indicate the coats you brought)*, but God made fur coats for the animals. People can make dolls out of paper or plastic, but only God can make boys and girls.

Let's thank God for our coats to keep us warm in this cold weather. Let's thank Him too for making the sun and the snow and the rain. Let's thank Him for making you and me. Let's thank Him for creating everything in such a wise and wonderful way.

7 Creed

Object: An American flag and the Bible

Concept: A creed is a summary of all that we believe.

Text: The Apostle's Creed

How many of you boys and girls go to school? *(Count the hands raised.)* In the corner of the classroom or on the wall near the front of the room, there are flags like this one. *(Hold up the flag.)* Sometimes we pledge allegiance to the flag. *(Place your hand over your heart and look at the flag.)* We put our right hands over our hearts and say the pledge. When we do this, we promise to obey the laws of the land. We say that we love our country. We say this to the flag because the flag stands for our country. The flag isn't the United States of America, is it? We may pretend that we are talking to our president and to our country when we talk to the flag. The flag is something that is small enough for us to hold and to have in our classrooms. The United States is too big to see all at once so we use the flag to stand for our country.

The church is very big too. We come to church and hear lots of sermons. We have many Sunday school lessons. All of these come from the Bible *(hold up the Bible)*. There are lots and lots of important things in this book. It is God's Word and we must read and study it often to learn more and more of what God has to say.

But suppose that one of your friends asked you what the Bible says. What are you going to say? *(Hold up the Bible again.)* Look at this Bible. It is a big book with many, many pages. That means it is going to be very hard to tell your friend everything about it. There's just too much to say. Even ministers who study the Bible all their lives can't learn it all.

But we do have some help. A long time ago someone wrote a little summary of what the Bible says. He tried to put down all the most important things about our faith. We call this a creed. The creed is short enough so that we can easily learn it by heart.

When you hear your moms and dads and brothers and sisters say the creed in church today, they are saying that they believe what the Bible says. You can learn the creed and say it too. The creed is a short way of saying what the Bible teaches. That's just like the little flag which stands for the great big United States of America.

So if someone asks you what the Bible says, just tell him the Apostles' Creed. In that way you will tell him the most important things that the Bible teaches.

8 Death

Object: A stone and a small house plant
Concept: Death is the gateway to heaven for those who love God.
Text: *I Corinthians 15:54, 55* "Death is swallowed up in victory. O death, where is thy victory?"

In one hand I have this cold, hard rock. In the other there is this nice green plant *(demonstrate both objects)*. Who can tell me which of these is alive? *(Allow time for answers from the children.)* Of course. The stone isn't alive. It's cold. It doesn't grow bigger or change color. But the plant is alive. It grows and has some pretty little flowers. A cold stone just won't grow even if we give it water and put it in the warm sunshine.

Some day this plant will die. It will stop growing bigger. When it is dead it will turn brown and dry up.

People die too. Sometimes they get very sick and die. Sometimes people die because of a bad car accident. Our grandfathers and grandmothers die when they get very old. We all will die someday, too.

Death isn't a nice thing to talk about because it makes us very sad. If a good friend dies, we are very sad. He is no longer with us. We can't play with him. Jesus' disciples were also very sad when the soldiers killed Jesus on the cross. They thought they had lost a good friend and their teacher. But, of course, Jesus didn't stay dead.

Many people are afraid of dying. They're scared because they don't know what will happen to them after they die. Did you know that the pharoahs of Egypt buried soldiers with them in the ground because they thought they would need protection after death?

The Bible tells us that we really don't have to be scared of death. Boys and girls, do you know where we go after we die, if we love God? *(Allow time for response.)* You're right! We go to heaven to be with Jesus.

When you go home today, try to see how many things along the road or sidewalk are dead. How many are alive? Then remember that someday maybe someone we love very much will die. We will die one day too. But if we love Jesus, death is like a doorway. We can walk through it into heaven where we will live with Jesus and never be sad again. We will be in a very beautiful place with Jesus forever. When we die, we won't be like this stone *(hold the stone high)* but we will be alive in heaven.

9 Disciple

Object: A nursery rhyme book with the rhyme "Mary Had a Little Lamb"

Concept: A disciple is a student and a follower.

Text: *Luke 9:23* "If any man would come after me, let him deny himself and take up his cross daily and follow me."

Boys and girls, I'm going to read you the nursery rhyme called, "Mary had a little lamb." *(Read the rhyme slowly and clearly.)* That is a nice little rhyme and I am sure that many of you know it by heart.

Sheep are animals that like to follow a leader. They will follow a shepherd wherever the shepherd may go. Sheep never like to be the leaders. In fact some people say that a goat can lead the sheep right into the building where the sheep will be killed for meat. The sheep don't ask questions. They just go where they are led.

Mary's little lamb was a good sheep. It followed Mary to school. That lamb didn't think about the children who were laughing at it. The lamb wanted to be near Mary. So the lamb went into the school building.

We are something like sheep. We like to follow other leaders. If we play musical instruments, we must follow the conductor. At school we follow our teacher. But most important, Jesus wants us to follow Him.

He wants us to be His disciples. That means that He wants us to listen to Him and go wherever He wants us to go.

Jesus chose twelve men to be His special followers. They were Peter, Andrew, James, John, Philip, Bartholomew, Thomas, Matthew, another James, Thaddaeus, Simon, and Judas. These men were Jesus' disciples. They followed Jesus everywhere. The disciples listened carefully to Jesus as He preached. The twelve men saw Jesus' miracles. Jesus even had special lessons for the disciples to learn.

We can be Jesus' disciples too. When we follow Jesus, we must listen to what He says to us in the Bible. We must obey Him. Sometimes other boys and girls may wonder why we go to church. We can explain that Jesus wants us to go to church on Sunday, and we want to follow His commands. We want to obey Him.

10 Discipline

Object: A piece of wood and some sandpaper
Concept: God often must discipline us because He loves us and wants us to be good.
Text: *Hebrews 12:7* "God is treating you as sons; for what son is there whom his father does not discipline?"

I am going to pretend that I am a carpenter. I have a piece of wood that has just been cut. The edge is still very rough. *(Call a child forward to feel the wood you have in your hand.)* Be careful! Don't get any slivers in your hand. The board is rough, isn't it? *(Allow the child to respond.)*

If a piece of wood is rough, we must make it smooth. We can't use rough wood when we build a chair. It would hurt to sit in a rough chair! So I take a piece of sandpaper *(hold up the sheet of sandpaper).* The sandpaper is also rough. But when I sand the edge of the wood, then all of a sudden the wood becomes smooth. Feel the edge now. *(Have the same child feel the edge.)* Is it smooth or rough? *(Allow the child to report.)*

Sometimes we are a little like a rough piece of wood. We do bad things that make other people sad. Maybe we tell a lie about one of our friends. If we say angry words to our parents, they are not pleased with us. When we do these bad things, then we are like a rough piece of wood that gives slivers. Slivers of wood hurt our fingers. And angry words and lies also hurt our friends and our parents.

God doesn't want us to be like rough boards. He sometimes sends troubles to sand us down and smooth our rough spots. He disciplines us because He wants us to be good. He wants us to learn the right way to live. Our parents discipline us for the same reason.

When God or our parents discipline us, the punishment may hurt a lot. God also loves us and wants us to learn to obey Him. The Israelites learned to obey God when God disciplined them.

The Israelites many times had worshiped false gods. This displeased God very much. God disciplined His people by sending armies from other countries to bother the people. Then the Israelites realized how much they needed God to protect them. So, through the rough times the Israelites learned that God wanted them to obey and love Him.

We must also learn that God disciplines us to teach us to be good. He does this because He loves us. God's discipline may be rough like sandpaper. But rough sandpaper makes a piece of wood smooth and beautiful.

If your parents discipline you, it is because they love you. Sometimes it will be hard to remember that. But just think about the rough sandpaper which makes a board very smooth *(sand the wood as you speak the last sentences)*.

11 Doubt

Object: A small closed box with a blue marble, a jack and a stick of gum inside

Concept: Doubt goes away when we really believe.

Text: *John 20:25* ". . . Unless I see in his hands the print of the nails, and place my finger in the mark of the nails, and place my hand in his side, I will not believe."

Listen to this, boys and girls. *(Rattle the box with a blue marble, a jack and a stick of gum inside.)* Do you wonder what I have in here? *(Rattle it again.)* If I told you I had a blue marble, a jack, and a stick of gum inside, would you believe me? *(Most will say 'yes'. Hopefully some will say 'no'. Now talk to those who said 'no'.)* You don't believe that I have all those things in this box? How can I prove to you that those things are really inside? Would you believe me if I opened the box and let you look at them? *(Wait for responses of 'yes'.)* That's the only way you will really believe that there's a blue marble, a jack and a stick of gum inside? Then after the service, you may come up and look, to take all your doubts away.

Doubts are strange things, aren't they? We often say, "I doubt it" or "I won't believe it until I see it."

The Bible tells us about a man that we sometimes call the Doubter. His name was Thomas—one of the twelve disciples. He knew that Jesus had died on the cross. He knew Jesus had the marks from the nails in His hands and feet. He knew too that the Roman soldier had stuck his spear into Jesus' side.

And now his friends, the other disciples, said, "Jesus is alive, we saw Him!" But Thomas was a doubter. He had to have proof. He said he wouldn't believe such an amazing story unless he actually saw the hands and feet of Jesus with the marks of the nails in them. He even wanted to touch the place on Jesus' side where it had been pierced with the sword—then and then only would Thomas believe.

The living Jesus appeared to Thomas and showed Thomas His hands and feet. Jesus even asked Thomas to put his hand on the place where the spear had pierced Jesus' side. And then all of his doubts disappeared. He really knew and he really believed. Jesus told him, "Thomas, because you have seen me, you believe."

Then Jesus gave us a promise. He said, "Blessed are those who have not seen and yet believe."

Whenever we have doubts about whether or not Jesus is really alive, all we have to do is remember Thomas. He was a doubter. He wanted proof and Jesus gave him that proof so we can believe. We serve a living Savior. There's no doubt about it!

12 Eternity

Object: An alarm clock and a calendar
Concept: A Christian will be forever with God.
Text: *Psalm 90:4* "For a thousand years in thy sight are but as yesterday when it is past, or as a watch in the night."

Boys and girls, who can tell me what time of the morning it is on this alarm clock? *(Hold up the alarm clock and allow the children to respond.)* Very good! Now how long will it be before you will eat your lunch? *(Again allow the children to respond.)* Maybe that was a little hard to figure out but I'm sure that most of us will be eating in about _____hours, when the hands of the alarm clock will be at twelve o'clock. *(Calculate the number of hours until noon and move the hands of the clock to read twelve o'clock.)*

When we talk about hours and minutes we are talking about time. Clocks like this alarm clock *(hold it up)* tell us time. If we want to know what time it is, we look at the clock. The watch that I have on my arm *(point to it)* is a little clock. It is just like this big alarm clock because it also tells the time.

An alarm clock makes noise when we have to get up. If we have to get up at seven o'clock in the morning, we can set the alarm for that time. We don't know what time it is when we sleep. The alarm clock knows that. When it is seven o'clock sharp the alarm goes off *(operate the clock so as to engage the alarm).* It's loud, isn't it? As we wake up we know what time it is. It's time to get ready for school.

A calendar is like an alarm clock. This calendar tells us that the month is _____ *(insert the correct month).* It tells us time too but it's a long time. Years are a long time too. If your grandfather is ninety years old, he has lived a long, long time. The Bible tells us your grandfather will die some day, and we will too. Then what happens?

God tells us that if we love Jesus, then we will be with God forever. That's a long, long time. That's eternity. Eternity is such a long time that we won't even need alarm clocks or calendars *(put the objects aside).* We will be with Jesus for eternity.

If your moms and dads tell you that in two months you're going to visit your grandfather, that will be fun. Vacation from school is in _____ months *(insert the correct number).* But just remember that if we· love Jesus, then we know that we will be with Him for eternity. That isn't nine months; it isn't nine years; it isn't ninety years; it's forever.

13 Faith

Object: Picture of a large bridge or a model bridge made of a board
from one chair to another with a toy car to push across
Concept: Faith in Jesus is like a bridge that connects man to God.
Text: *Hebrews 11:1* "Now faith is the assurance of things hoped for,
the conviction of things not seen."

When the early pioneers moved west in their covered wagons, there were no roads to follow. As they traveled over land, they got along quite well until they came to a swift river or deep canyon. Then they needed a way to get to the other side.

Sometimes they would build a bridge. They would cut down trees and build beams. They would drive down pillars and tie logs and planks together to make a roadway. What hard work it must have been to build such early bridges.

Today we have engineers to design our bridges. They build high bridges across deep canyons. Strong bridges are built to carry railroad trains or many lanes of cars and busses at once. The Brooklyn bridge has six lanes for cars on top and a second layer to carry busses. We have long bridges like the Oakland Bay Bridge that is over eight miles long.

Hikers who climb high mountains need to watch out for deep crevices in the ice. Sometimes these crevices will have snow bridges on top of them, which hide the danger. If the hiker tries to cross the crevice on the snow bridge, it may cave in. Bridges can be dangerous if they are not strong enough to get you from one side to the other. *(Point to the two ends of the bridge on the picture or push the little car across the model bridge you have made.)*

All of these bridges have one purpose. They allow people to get from one side of the stream or canyon to the other.

Ever since Adam and Eve sinned, there has been a deep canyon between people, who are sinners, and God, who is holy and perfect. People have tried to build many kinds of bridges to heaven. Some have tried to build the bridge of good works. Some have tried to get across with the bridges of false religions. Some, like Evel Knievel, try to jump across without a bridge. But false bridges and our own efforts won't get us across the canyon of sin. They won't carry us across to God and to heaven.

There is only one way to get to heaven, and that is through faith in the Lord Jesus Christ. He is the bridge between God and man. Many Christians have already crossed into heaven by faith. Hebrews 11 tells us of Abel and Enoch, of Noah and Abraham, of Issac and Jacob, of Moses and Gideon and David and many, many others. The bridge of faith in Jesus is strong enough to carry us all. It will never cave in like a snow bridge. It has no rotting timbers or rusting cables like old bridges. The bridge of faith in Jesus never grows old. He is the same yesterday, today and forever (Heb. 13:8). Put your faith in Him because He alone is the bridge to heaven.

14 The Fall

Object: An egg, a glass bowl
Concept: The "Fall" into sin shattered the image of God in man, but the image of God, though shattered, is still there.
Text: *Colossians 3:9, 10* "Do not lie to one another, seeing that you have put off the old nature with its practices and have put on the new nature, which is being renewed in knowledge after the image of its creator."

Did you eat an egg for breakfast? *(Hold up an egg.)* Many people have eggs for breakfast. Some like boiled eggs, some like fried eggs, some like scrambled eggs. But before you can eat an egg, you have to do something. You have to break the shell.

(Pick up the glass bowl in the other hand and hold both the egg and bowl in view of the audience.) Now if I take my egg and drop it into the bowl, it would look very different, wouldn't it? Instead of being easy to hold, some of it would probably slip right through my fingers. Instead of having a nice whole smooth shell with the yoke and everything else inside in its place, it would be all mixed up. Just look. *(Drop the egg in the bowl from the height of about two feet and show the result.)*

That egg is something like we are, boys and girls. You know that when God created Adam and Eve, He made them good, perfect, and in the image of God Himself. God made man like Himself—to love and do what is right and true and kind.

Then sin came along. When Adam, the father of the whole human race, first fell into sin by disobeying God, it was like the egg falling into the bowl. And all of Adam's children and grand children and great-grand children, and great, great, great-grand children, and even everyone living on earth today—that includes you and me—have sinned too. People's lives were all mixed up. The perfect image of God in us was shattered like the egg in the bowl.

But when you look in my bowl, *(show it to the audience)* you can still see that what I have in here is an egg. It's all messed up, but it's still an egg. In the same way, people are still God's children, even after they fall into sin.

God still loves us. God sent His Son, Jesus, to save us. He gives us new hearts so we can love Him. It would take a miracle to put my broken egg back together, wouldn't it? It took a miracle to change our broken lives and make them whole again. It took the miracle of Jesus' love.

15 Good Works

Object: A little shrub or tree branch with some grapes, apples and bananas or other fruit fastened to it with wire
Concept: Christians do good works because they are thankful to God.
Text: *James 2:18* ". . . and I by my works will show you my faith."

Just for a little while, boys and girls, I would like to have you act like detectives. I would like to have you look at this little tree and see if you notice anything strange about it. Be sure to look as carefully as you can. Hold up your hand if you see anything wrong with it.

(Wait for pupil response.) Do you see something wrong, _____? What is it? *(Child will likely respond by saying that he sees grapes and apples or apples and bananas growing from the same tree.)* Good, _____! Who else sees something strange about my little tree? *(Again solicit some pupil's response to note the different types of fruit on the same tree.)* Right, _____! You see two different kinds of fruit growing on the same tree. Well, now, why is that so strange? *(Obtain responses that show that only one kind of fruit grows on a tree.)* Yes, apple trees have apples and grape vines have grapes. You can tell what kind of a tree it is if you just look to see what kind of fruit grows on it.

Do you know that the Bible says that you can tell something about people in the same way? You watch what people do. Just like you can

35

tell a tree by the kind of fruit it grows, you can tell a person's heart by what he does. If he does bad things all the time, you can pretty much tell what's in his heart. But if he does lots of good things, it tells you that he has kindness and goodness inside.

The Bible tells us that we should do good works—not because we need to pay for our sins, we never could do that. Jesus died on the cross to forgive all of our sins. We need to do good works to show Jesus how thankful we are for saving us. And, we want other people to know what kind of people we are inside. We can't have both bad works and good works as fruit in our lives any more than my little tree can produce both apples and grapes. If we are really Christians, we want our lives to have fruit. We surely don't want to be empty, with no fruit at all. And we don't want fruit of bad deeds either.

What we really want is just one kind of fruit—just good works that will show Jesus how much we love Him.

16 Gospel

Object: A newspaper with headlines in large print

Concept: The Good News of God is about Jesus as a free gift from God. (Christmas theme)

Text: *Luke 2:10* "Be not afraid, for behold, I bring you good news of a great joy which will come to all the people."

Every day a newspaper comes to our homes. *(The frequency may vary in some areas; some towns may have a weekly newspaper.)* I'm sure that one of the first things we look for is the comic strips. We all like to read the comics. *(Turn to this and other sections as you refer to them.)* But there's a lot more in the newspaper. There's the sports page. There's the part where the stores try to sell their toys or their food. And there's the most important part. The section at the front of the newspaper gives us the news. We see what is happening in the world. We can also read about what is going on in our own city.

Let's look at this newspaper. We can read this headline for us? *(Point out the most easily read headline.)* Do you think that the headline talks about good news or is it about bad news? *(Give opportunity for an opinion or two.)* Look at this one. *(Point out a headline which obviously refers to some good news and read it aloud.)* Is this good news or bad? *(Again allow for an opinion.)*

The bad news in our newspapers makes us feel sad, doesn't it? We don't want bad things to happen. We don't want somebody's house to burn down. Headlines that bring good news make us happy. That's why we call stories about happy things "good news." The Bible also has good news. In some ways the Bible is like a newspaper that gives us stories that can make us happy.

The shepherds at Christmas time were the first people to hear the good news of Jesus' birth. They were taking care of their sheep on the hills near Bethlehem. But all of a sudden there was a bright light in the sky. There were angels all around them who told the shepherds some good news. Jesus, the Savior of the world, was born in the little town of Bethlehem. This made the shepherds so happy that they left their sheep and ran into Bethlehem to see Jesus.

The Bible gives us the good news about Jesus. This good news is the gospel. It is the good news of God which tells us that Jesus is our Savior. This should make us very happy. Jesus is God's free gift to us. That's the best news that anyone can read.

A newspaper has the comics and sports news. Its news can be good or it can be bad. The Bible is like a newspaper (hold up the newspaper). It tells us the best news in the whole world. The news of the Bible is better than the news this newspaper could ever give.

We can read this paper (hold it up) for the news of the world. But remember that the Bible gives us the gospel. It is the good news of a free gift from God. We should read it every day just like we read our newspapers every day.

17 Grace

Object: Your paycheck
Concept: Grace is God's free, unearned love to His children.
Text: *Romans 11:6* "But if it is by grace, it is no longer on the basis of works; otherwise grace would no longer be grace."

Boys and girls, did you ever get paid for doing something? Suppose, girls, that you and your mother would agree that every time you did the dishes, you would earn a nickel. Or, boys, suppose you would make a deal with your dad that every time you swept the garage or mowed the lawn you would get a dime or quarter.

Then if you did the work you had agreed to do and got paid for it, you have earned the money, right? Older boys and girls get jobs baby-sitting, delivering newspapers or picking berries. (*Add the kind of work done by boys and girls in your community.*) In each case, when they get paid, they get the money they have earned.

Grownups do that too. People get jobs and when they do their work and earn their wages, they get paid. Did you know that I get paid too? Look, here is my paycheck (*hold it up*). To earn my paycheck, I study a lot and get my sermons ready for the church. I go to visit those who are sick. I take care of funerals and weddings. I meet with the church council and go to lots of other meetings. (*Add any special requirements that you are expected to fulfill.*) And when I do my work, I get paid.

It's nice to earn something, isn't it? It gives us a good feeling when we get paid for what we do.

But the Bible tells us that there is one thing, one very important thing, that we cannot earn, and that is our own salvation. The Bible says that we are saved only by grace. Being saved by grace means that we can't earn our way to heaven no matter how hard we work or what we do. God gives us salvation just because He loves us.

So grace is something like getting paid for something you didn't or couldn't do. Suppose that you got sick and couldn't do the dishes. Or suppose that you broke your leg and couldn't mow the lawn. What if your parents did the work for you, and gave you the nickel or dime anyway? What would you do? Well, the only thing that you could do would be to say, "thank you."

And that's what we can do and that's what we must do to God. He sent His Son into the world to die on the cross and earn the salvation that we couldn't earn for ourselves. Don't forget to say, "Thank You" in your prayers to God for His grace.

18 Guilt

Object: A dirty old rag made from an old white shirt, an old pail
Concept: Even man's best works are imperfect and, apart from the salvation we have in Christ, we are guilty before God.
Text: *Isaiah 64:6* "And all our righteousnesses are as filthy rags. . . ." (KJV)

The janitor knows what this is—it's his old mop pail and inside is an old rag. (*Hold up the dirty rag. Let a little dirty water drip out of it as you hold it above the pail to add to the "dirty" effect.*) Do you know what this old rag used to be? A nice clean white shirt. Well, it doesn't look much like that now. It's only a filthy rag!

In the Bible the prophet Isaiah talks about filthy rags. He says all our righteousness is like a filthy rag. He says that even our best works are dirty with sin. That's not very good is it?

Think of a stream that starts out in the mountains. At first, it's crystal clear from the melting snow or a fresh spring. But before long the sewage of the city and the garbage of people gets thrown in and the stream gets all polluted. That's what we're like without Jesus' saving grace. We're guilty before God.

We're guilty because we've broken God's law. We deserve only His punishment. Even our very best works won't save us. To God, they just look like this old rag. There really isn't anything that we can do to save ourselves.

You know that the dirty rag in that bucket *(point to it)* can't wash itself. It can't jump out of the mop bucket and walk over into the washing machine, pour in some soap and make itself clean. No, if it's going to get clean, somebody else has to wash it.

That's the way that Jesus found us, guilty in our sins and unable to help ourselves. He died on the cross to wash us from our sins to make us clean. He has taken our guilt away; now we must live thankfully for Him.

19 Holy

Object: A Bible with the word *Holy* showing clearly in large print
Concept: God wants His people to be holy as He is holy—separated from sin.
Text: *I Peter 1:15* "... but as he who called you is holy, be holy yourselves in all your conduct. ..."

This book I am holding in my hand is the most important book in all the world, boys and girls. It is called the Bible. It was written by many different people like Moses and Joshua, David and Daniel, Luke and Paul. There were thirty-six people in all who were told by the Holy Spirit to write parts of the Bible. The first part *(hold up your Bible and indicate the Old Testament)* is the Old Testament, which was written before Jesus was born. The second part *(indicate the New Testament section)* is called the New Testament, which tells about how Jesus came to earth to save us from our sins and how we can serve Him.

But when you look at the name of this book carefully, it doesn't just say the word *Bible* on it all by itself. In front of the word *Bible* is the word *Holy*. It really says, "Holy Bible."

Do you know what *holy* means? We use the word *holy* when we talk about God and the things of God. The word *holy* means separated from sin and set apart for God's service.

The Bible is holy because it contains God's holy and perfect message for us. No other book in the world is holy. The Bible is God's book— God's Word to us.

When we say the Apostle's Creed, we say; "I believe in the holy catholic church." That means that we believe that church members around the world like you and me are to be separated from sin for God's service.

The angels in heaven praise God for His holiness for He is perfect and without sin. They sing "Holy, Holy, Holy, Lord God Almighty." We can praise God, too, when we sing about God's holiness.

The Bible tells us in I Peter 1:15 (hold up Bible to place and read) "As he who called you is holy, be holy yourselves in all your conduct . . ."

That means that we must try to be pure and separate ourselves from sin just as God is pure and holy and is separated from sin. If other boys and girls are planning to do something wrong, remember that God wants us to separate ourselves from things that are sinful and not take part.

We all need to be reminded that God wants us to be holy like He is holy. Every time you see a Bible or hear it read, remember that the word holy (point to it on the Bible you are holding) is there because the Bible tells about our holy God who wants us to be like Him.

20 Humility

Object: A feather
Concept: God humbles the proud.
Text: *James 4:10* "Humble yourselves before the Lord and he will exalt you."

Isn't this a pretty feather? I think it came from a _____ (*use the name of the bird from which your feather came and wave it a bit in the air*). You know, feathers can be very beautiful. A peacock's feather is long with lots of colors. Some feathers are black, some are pure white. Others have many colors. Feathers help a bird to fly. They keep the bird warm when the weather is cold, and keep him dry when it rains. But this feather reminds me of a Bible story.

It reminds me of the great King Nebuchadnezzar. He lived in the great city of Babylon with its huge wall and its beautiful hanging gardens. Well, one night, the king had a dream and nobody but Daniel could tell what it meant. It was about a great tree that reached to heaven. The birds lived in its branches and the animals found shade under it. But the tree was cut down; only the stump was left.

Daniel explained that the tree in the dream stood for King Nebuchadnezzar, who was very proud. He had to be made humble. Daniel said that was why the tree was cut down to a stump in the dream.

Daniel predicted that unless the king started honoring God, his kingdom would be taken away.

Eventually, the dream came true. One day, the proud king was walking on the roof of his palace looking at the beautiful city. He said, "Is not this great Babylon which I have built by my mighty power. . . ?" Nebuchadnezzar took all of the credit. He did not admit that God had given him the great city.

But God humbled the proud king. Since Nebuchadnezzar didn't honor God, he began to be mixed up inside. His mind became confused. He had to leave the palace and the beautiful city. He began to live like an animal in the fields. His fingernails became like birds' claws and his hair grew as long as eagles' feathers. *(Again, hold up the feather in your hand.)*

As the king became humble, he began to think clearly again. He realized how important it was to praise God instead of praising himself. So God gave the kingdom back to Nebuchadnezzar.

Every time you see a feather like this, won't you think of the proud king and what happened to him? In the Bible, God tells us that he wants His children to be humble and not to be proud. Jesus was an example for us. He humbled Himself when He left His throne of glory in heaven and came to earth to suffer and to die on the cross for our sins. He washed the feet of His disciples to teach them and to teach us that we should be humble. We should be willing to do the lowest tasks for one another.

The next time you are tempted to feel proud, remember King Nebuchadnezzar and how important it is to praise God instead of ourselves.

21 Immortality

Object: A dried ear of corn. Remove several kernels and plant them in a small flower pot. Use the sprouts for this object lesson when they are three or four inches high.

Concept: Man must die before he can truly live.

Text: *I Corinthians 15:53* "For this perishable nature must put on the imperishable, and this mortal nature must put on immortality."

Boys and girls, you know what this is, don't you? *(Hold up dry ear of corn.)* Yes, it's an ear of corn with lots and lots of kernels on it. If I take out one little kernel like this *(do so and hold it up)* I can look at it and say, "What good is one little kernel?" I could just as well throw it away.

But I didn't throw away the kernels I took off. I just took a few of them and planted them in this pot of ground. And you see what happened? *(Hold up your little plants.)* They have already started to grow.

Now if I give them time to grow up to be big corn plants, they will have ears of corn with hundreds of kernels and if I planted all those, they would all have ears of corn with thousands and thousands of kernels of corn. All from a single little kernel like this! *(Hold up one kernel.)*

But something needs to happen to my kernel of corn before it can grow into a new corn plant. Do you know what it is? *(Wait for* responses—such as "put it in the ground" or "bury it".) Yes, that's right; I have to plant it in the ground. I have to bury it, and when the new little plant so full of life grows up, the old, hard, dry kernel disappears. Only when the old kernel dies and disappears can a new corn plant begin to grow.

Jesus used an example like this when He was talking to His disciples. They wanted to know more about immortality, that is, more about eternal life. Jesus explained that dying was something like planting a seed. He said in John 12:24, "Truly, truly, I say to you, unless a grain of wheat falls into the earth and dies, it remains alone; but if it dies, it bears much fruit." He meant that a new and living plant comes out of a seed that is buried in the ground. A person who dies is buried in the grave but out of that body the soul comes and lives a new spiritual life that never dies.

If the kernel of grain was never planted in the ground, no new plant would grow. Only when we die and are buried will we begin our heavenly lives that will never end. That will be a time of eternal pain and punishment for those who don't have Jesus as their Savior. It will be a time of eternal joy and praise for those who love and serve Him, for those who believe in Him.

Death for the Christian is only the beginning of eternal life with Jesus. When you wonder about death, think of the new little plants that came up from the seeds that I put in the ground. (Hold up your little plants again.) They are carrying on the life of the corn plant and starting to grow all over again.

22 Infinite

Object: A short (24") piece of string, a longer (48") piece of string, a roll of twine, a ruler

Concept: We measure short and long things, big and small things, but God cannot be measured.

Text: *Psalm 145:3* "Great is the Lord, and greatly to be praised, and his greatness is unsearchable."

Boys and girls, the short string that I have in my hand now is about two feet long. *(Hold up the string by one end.)* This little piece couldn't tie up a very big box, could it? It's just too short. But now let me take this longer piece of string. *(Take the 48" string.)* Who can tell me which of these two strings is the longer string? *(Hold the two pieces near to each other and allow the children to respond.)* Of course this one *(hold the longer one a little higher than the other)* is longer. It can tie up a box.

Now I will hold up these first two pieces of string next to this long, long one. This short piece stops here *(point out the end of the string).* This longer one goes all the way down to here *(again point out the end).* But look at this long, long, long string! *(Hold up the end from the roll of string as high as possible leaving the other end in the roll on the floor.)* We can't even see the end of this string because it's so long.

We can measure these two strings *(measure the two shorter lengths)*. This one *(the shorter length)* is twenty-four inches long, and this one *(the longer one)* is forty-eight inches long. However, we can't measure the longest one now. It's simply too long for that.

I can take this ruler and I can measure you too. Some of you are short like this little string and some of you are bigger like the longer string. But only God is like this long, long string. We can't measure God because He's too big. He's infinite. We can't hold a ruler up and measure God.

The Bible tells us that God is infinite. God is so big that He made the world. He made you and me. There is even a song that says, "He's got the whole world in his hands!"

Sometimes we feel a little scared when we can't see our moms and dads. But when we do see them, then we feel safe. They are bigger than we are and can help us. They can do lots of things that we can't do.

God is so powerful and infinite that He can help us even more than our parents. God can always help us. I can't even tell you how big God is. He is something like this long, long string. We can't measure Him. But the Bible says that even though we can't know how big God is, God will always help us if we pray to Him.

23 Inspiration

Object: A deflated balloon and the Bible
Concept: God breathed His words into the authors of the Bible.
Text: *II Timothy 3:16* "All scripture is inspired by God. . . ."

I'm sure that everybody likes to go to birthday parties. At lots of parties there are pretty decorations on the table and the walls. There is ice cream and candy and a cake with candles. And almost every birthday party has balloons of every shape and size. I have here a birthday balloon *(hold up the deflated balloon)*. Now what is the first thing that we must do to this balloon? *(Let the children respond.)* Of course, we must blow it up. When we blow it up like this *(inflate the balloon)*, we blow into the balloon. Now the little balloon is a big one because we blew into it.

The biggest balloon that was ever built was more than 800 feet tall. That balloon wasn't used for any birthday party but was used for a science experiment in New Mexico in 1966. That balloon also had to be blown up. It tooks lots of air to do that.

Sometimes we have to blow into a person's mouth if he's not breathing. It's just like blowing up a balloon. Only this time we are blowing air into his lungs to help him to breathe better. If he doesn't breathe, he will die. We blow up his lungs just like little balloons. When we do that we can save his life.

The Bible tells us that God did something like that when He helped men like Matthew, Mark, Luke, and John. God inspired them to write the Bible. He breathed into them the words to use. The Bible is such a special book that God helped His people to write it. It is so special, in fact, that God breathed into their hearts the words to use. That's how we got the Bible.

When you see a balloon at a birthday party, think about the Bible. Blowing up the balloon is something like the inspiration of the Bible. Let the balloon *(hold up the now-inflated balloon)* remind you that the Bible is very special because God inspired the people who wrote it. He breathed the words into their hearts. The Bible came by the inspiration *(make a blowing sound with your mouth)* of God.

24 Intercession

Object: Two lollipops

Concept: Intercession means to make entreaty on behalf of another. Just as Jesus prays for us, we are to pray for others.

Text: *Hebrews 7:25* "He is able for all time to save those who draw near to God through Him, since he always lives to make intercession for them."

Look at these two lollipops. They remind me of something I saw the other day in the barbershop. A boy about four years old was getting his haircut. He was so good and sat so still that when the barber was finished he gave the boy a lollipop. He was just going to put the lollipop box back under the counter when the little boy said, "My little sister is at home and she never gets a haircut at the barbershop. Can I have a lollipop for her too?" The barber asked the little boy how old his sister was. The boy said she was almost two years old but couldn't talk as well as he could. Then the barber asked the boy if he liked his little sister and he said, "Yes, most of the time, and I would like a lollipop for her, too." Then the barber let him pick one out of the box. I'm sure that the little girl was happy that her brother had been so thoughtful.

Do any of you have a little brother or sister that you would like to give a lollipop to? *(Wait for a hand to be raised, then call the child up to the front.)* "Who would you like to give a lollipop to?" *(Wait for child's response.)* Do you like_____? Well give one to him/her and you may have the other one for yourself. *(Child may return to his seat.)*

It is nice, boys and girls, to ask for something for someone else, isn't it? When Peter was in prison, all the members of the church gathered together and prayed for Peter's safety. They weren't praying for themselves, they were praying for Peter. We call this intercession. Intercession is when we pray for somebody else.

If you pray for your father and mother, or if they pray for you, we call this intercessory prayer. Christians should pray a lot, but not just for themselves. They should also pray for others.

Jesus is the great intercessor. Hebrews 7:25 tells us that He always lives to make intercession for us.

Sometimes we are in a hurry and we just forget to pray for others. But Jesus never forgets to intercede for us.

The little boy's sister couldn't talk very well yet, so he asked the barber for a lollipop for her. Like the little girl, we don't really know how to pray as we should, but the Holy Spirit takes our feeble little prayers and adds to them. He makes them perfect and brings them to God's throne of grace. So don't get discouraged because you can't pray as well as you would like to. And don't forget to pray for others.

25 Justification

Object: A flat board ½" x 2" x 12" or a ruler
Concept: God punished His own Son and said that the sinner was innocent.
Text: *Romans 3:28* "For we hold that a man is justified by faith apart from works of the law."

Look at this board! *(Grip it in your hand.)* It looks quite hard and strong. If you did a bad thing, your dad or mom might come to you with this. What do you think they would do with it? *(Allow one or two children to respond.)* You're right! They might spank you with it. That would hurt, but it would punish you for something your dad or mom didn't want you to do. You disobeyed them and so they spank you with their hand or with a board like this. *(Hold the board and slap it against your hand once or twice.)*

(Call a child forward—one that is older and will not be frightened.) Let's say that_____ *(use the child's name)* did not obey me and I was going to spank him. Let's just say that he was bad and deserves to be punished. Now instead of spanking *(name)* I spank myself *(go through the action.)* At the same time I say that *(name)* is innocent. He won't get a spanking any more. He did wrong but instead I was spanked with this board *(hold it up again)* in his place and he goes free. I bet that *(name)* would be happy. Would you be happy,

__(name)__ ? You'd be happy and free from punishment because you were justified. *(Have child return to his seat.)*

God does something like that when He justifies you and me. The Bible says that we aren't very good. We do all sorts of bad things, and God says that we must be punished. But, surprise! God punished Jesus instead. He punished His own Son Jesus, who never sinned. That's just how much God loves us. He sent His only son, His *beloved* son, to die in our place. When He justifies us He says that we aren't guilty of doing bad things. But He says that only because Jesus was once willing to be punished in our place.

I don't think any of us would want to be spanked for something that our brother or sister did. Would you like that? *(Let children respond.)* In fact, I think that we would all be very angry at our brother or sister if we were punished for something that they did. It just wouldn't be fair. But Jesus loved us so much that He didn't get angry. He wanted to do it. We are justified because He took our punishment for us.

Justification is a big word, I know, but it's something that is very wonderful. We can be very happy because God punished Jesus instead of punishing us. I hope that your dad and mom don't have to punish you or spank you with a board like this one *(hold it up again)*. But if they sometimes do have to punish you, it's probably because you have been bad. Just remember that God punished Jesus for something that you and I did. Because He suffered for us, we don't have to worry about being punished. We're free. We are justified. We should thank God for that. Isn't God wonderful?

26 Law

Object: A mirror
Concept: God's law is like a mirror that shows us what we are really like.
Text: *James 1:23-25* ". . . he is like unto a man beholding his natural face in a mirror; for he beholdeth himself, and goeth away, and straightway forgetteth what manner of man he was. But he that looketh into the perfect law, the law of liberty, and so continueth, being not a hearer that forgetteth but a doer that worketh, this man shall be blessed in his doing" (ASV).

This is really a windy morning, isn't it! Did you notice that as people came into church from the parking lot, they tried to hold their hair down a little so it wouldn't blow around so much? Then when the people got inside, you could see some of them trying to smooth their hair down or comb it a little.

When your hair gets all blown around, you can get it quite smooth again by just rubbing it down with your hand but you aren't quite sure what it's like until you look in a mirror like this *(hold up your mirror and look into it)*. Then you can see just where your hair is sticking up or is out of place.

Mirrors can tell you what you look like. I remember a story I read a long time ago about a little boy who lived in Africa. The people of his village didn't have any mirrors and one day he was playing by a pool of water. It was quiet and there were no ripples. He leaned over the water and suddenly he saw his reflection. It scared him so much he ran away. It was the first time he had ever seen himself.

The Bible tells us that God's law is like a mirror. Paul says, "I had not known sin, except through the law" (Rom. 7:7). When I look at God's law, I see myself as God sees me. He asks me to love Him above all. He asks me to honor my parents, He asks me not to steal or to hate or to covet.

I may have some jam on my face from breakfast time and I probably wouldn't notice it until I looked in my mirror and then I would see it right away. When I hear God's law, it's like looking in a mirror because then right away I see all the things God wants me to do that I didn't do.

If my mirror shows me my hair is mixed up, I can comb it straight. If it shows me my face is dirty, I can wash it. When God's law shows me I have sinned, I must remember to come to Jesus to ask His forgiveness.

27 The Lord's Supper

Concept: The Lord's Supper is a sacrament that helps us remember what Jesus did for us on the cross.

Text: *I Corinthians 11:24b* "This do in remembrance of me" (KJV).

Object: A "One Way" road sign made of cardboard similar to this model:

If your family has a car, your parents probably use it for going to work, doing the shopping, and for vacation. Maybe you rode in it to church today. Some day you will be able to drive a car just like your big brothers and sisters. It isn't very hard to learn how to drive it, but it is very important that we know all about the car. We must also know what traffic lights mean and why there are a lot of different signs along the side of the road.

If we see a "No Parking" sign, do you think that we should put our car in that place? *(Let the children respond.)* If the traffic light is red, it means we must stop. If we don't, we might hit another car. *(Hold up the "One Way" sign.)* This sign I have in my hand says, "One Way." When this sign is placed along a road, it means that all cars must go in the direction that the arrow shows. This sign tells us that we must go only in the right direction or our car will get into an accident.

The Lord's Supper really has two signs in it. They are the bread and the wine. *(Point out these items if used at a communion service.)* They are like this "One Way" sign that I have in my hand. They point us in the right direction. They show us the right place to look.

The bread and the wine remind us that Jesus died on the cross. The soldiers who crucified Jesus did terrible things to Him. They put nails into Jesus' hands and the blood ran out. The soldiers hurt His body and Jesus died. But He died so that you and I could be very happy, so that we can have eternal life. If we believe that Jesus loves us and if we love Him too, then we will be with Him always.

The bread and the wine on the communion table tell us, "Remember what Jesus did for you." The bread reminds us that His body was given for us. The wine reminds us that His blood was shed for us. He died so that we might live. Like this sign *(hold up the sign)* the bread and wine point in the right direction. They point straight to Jesus. The bread and the wine are like little arrows that show us how much Jesus really loves us.

28 Love

Object: A small toy car that must be wound up and runs with a spring

Concept: Love is the motivating force that impels us to obey Jesus' commandments.

Text: *II Corinthians 5:14* "For the love of Christ controls us. . . ."

This little toy car (*or other toy with wheels*) is lots of fun to play with. It looks just like a real car. It has a steering wheel and a windshield; it even has a tiny trunk that opens and a speedometer (*hold up and describe the one you have to show*).

But when you play with most toy cars and trucks there's just one problem. You have to push them everywhere they go. If you don't push them, they just stand still. But this little car is different. Over here on the side is a place where you can wind it up (*do so*). Now if I set it down, it will run by itself. Just watch (*let the toy car run across the stage or platform*). When I wound up the spring, the car ran without anybody pushing it. Pretty soon the spring winds down though, and the little car stops. It stands still again until somebody pushes it or winds it up again.

Some boys and girls are a lot like this little toy car. They don't do anything unless somebody gives them a push or winds them up. Just suppose that your mom or dad asks you to do something. Does it take a little push to get you started? Or do you have a spring inside of you that gets you started by yourself?

Love inside of your heart is like a spring in a toy car. Love makes you obey when your parents ask you to do something. Love makes you want to do what they ask you to do. They don't have to push you to get you started.

Jesus said, "If you love me, keep my commandments" (John 14:15). Love is like a spring that makes you want to do what Jesus wants you to do.

The spring in this little toy car *(hold it up again)* needs to be wound up to make the car go but very soon it will run down and stop. But love doesn't stop. Instead it grows stronger and stronger. If you really love Jesus you won't need a push to start doing His commandments and you won't slow down or stop. You'll always keep on trying to do what He wants you to do.

29 Mercy

Object: An imaginary fly
Concept: God shows mercy when we have every reason to expect harsh judgment.
Text: *Exodus 33:19* "I will make all my goodness pass before you, and will proclaim before you my name, 'The Lord' . . . [I] will show mercy on whom I will show mercy."

(Make some swatting motions about your head and look very annoyed.) Boys and girls, a fly is bothering me. He's buzzing around my head. Oh, what a pesky little thing. *(Hold very still for a second and say softly,)* There, now it's sitting on my nose and I'm going to catch him. *(Bring your hands near your nose.)* Easy does it. *(Make a grasping motion.)* Oh, I missed him! Ah, there he is again on my nose. *(Once again, make slow deliberate moves toward your nose.)* Go easy now! *(Make a sudden grasping motion.)* There I've got him! Now what should I do with him? *(Hold one hand in a closed fist as if to hold the fly.)*

Maybe I should kill this pesky fly. He deserves it because he was bothering me a lot. We all kill flies because they are dirty. They carry germs and sit on our food. But no, I don't think I will kill him. *(Begin to walk toward the window or door, whichever is the easiest to open.)* I think that I'll just let him go. He deserves to die, but I'll show mercy on him and let him go. *(Open the door or window, make a throwing motion and quickly close the door or window again.)* There, now he's gone.

In the Bible there's a story about Joseph who showed mercy on his brothers just like I showed mercy to the fly. Joseph's brothers were very bad. They didn't love Joseph. In fact, one day they sold him as a slave. What a terrible thing to do! They wanted to get rid of him forever. But after a long time Joseph became an important man in Egypt. He was almost as powerful as the king.

Then one day his brothers had to come to Egypt because they had to buy some food. They didn't have any food at home for their families. They were hungry and so they came to Joseph. They didn't know it was Joseph but Joseph knew them. Since he was such an important ruler, he could have punished them for the terrible things they had done to him. But Joseph didn't punish them. In fact, he gave them food freely. He even gave back their money. He showed mercy on his brothers.

God does something like that too. He shows mercy on us. The Bible says that God loved us so much that He sent His Son, Jesus. Jesus received our punishment and died on the cross for us. God shows us mercy and forgives us in Jesus' name.

I'm glad that that fly is gone. I don't like to have flies bothering me when I'm talking to you. The next time a fly bothers you I know that you'll want to get rid of it. But if you let the fly go just like I did then, you are showing mercy on that fly. Remember that this is what God does to you and me too. We deserve to be punished because of our sin. But God loves us so He lets us go free just like I did for the fly. God is wonderful, isn't He?

30 Obedience

Object: A list of excuses used by Bible characters as follows: Adam *(Gen. 3:12)*, Eve *(Gen. 3:13)*, Moses *(Exod. 4:10-13)*, Aaron *(Exod. 32:22-24)*

Text: *Romans 1:20* ". . . So they are without excuse."

When I was a boy, if I was absent from school, I had to bring a note from my father or mother the next day telling why I wasn't in class. The teacher would read the note and decide if it was a good reason or not. If it was a good reason, I was excused, and I didn't have to make up my school work. But if it wasn't an acceptable excuse, I was marked, "Unexcused" and I had to do all the assignments just as if I had been in class.

If people do what they are supposed to do, they don't need to make excuses. We make excuses most often when we fail to do something we should have done or when we disobey a rule. For example, if your parents ask you to do something, it's very easy to make an excuse for not doing it.

I wrote down a few excuses that you can find in the Bible. I will read them to you and you see if you can tell me who said it. Here is the first one:

"The woman who you gavest to be with me, she gave me fruit of the tree and I ate." Do you know whose excuse that was? *(Wait for the audience response.)* Yes, that was Adam's excuse for disobeying God.

Listen to this next excuse. "The serpent beguiled (tricked) me and I ate." Who used that excuse? *(Again, wait for audience response.)* That's right, it was Eve.

How about this one? "I am slow of speech and tongue; send some other person." *(If no one responds, give an added clue such as: God then sent his brother Aaron to go with him.)* Right, that was the excuse of Moses when God asked him to lead the people of Israel out of Egypt.

In Exodus 32:22-24 someone said, "You know the people, that they are set on evil. I said to them, Let any who have gold take it off, so they gave it to me and I threw it into the fire, and there came out this calf." Who made that excuse for not obeying God? *(Try to get some new respondents to this one. You may add this clue: It happened while Moses was up on Mt. Sinai.)* Yes, it was Aaron when he made the golden calf. He gave a ridiculous excuse for the idol that he made.

There are many other Bible characters who made excuses for not being obedient to God, and we sometimes make excuses, too. To be obedient is simply to do what we are asked to do. If we learn to obey we are on the path that God wants us to be on.

So the next time that you are tempted to make an excuse, stop! See if you can make the excuse unnecessary—be obedient instead!

31 Offerings

Object: A wash cloth and dishpan of water
Concept: God wants us to be cheerful givers.
Text: *II Corinthians 9:5* "I want it to be forthcoming as a generous gift, not as money wrung out of you" (Moffatt).

If your mother asks you to wash the dishes, she will probably give you a washcloth something like this one *(hold up the cloth)*. Then you dip it in the water *(do so)* and you're all ready to start. It's easy to get the cloth wet, but if you want to wipe off the table or the workbench, you don't want the cloth to be dripping wet *(hold up the dripping wet cloth)*. No, you squeeze out a little of the water by pinching it. *(Do so.)* Then if you want to get more water out, you have to twist it. *(Do so to get a little more out.)* The harder you twist, the more comes out.

Before there were automatic washing machines, our grandmothers and great-grandmothers had wringers on their old style washing machines. *(Display one if available.)* They pushed the wet clothes between two rollers and turned a crank that would squeeze the clothes to make some of the water come out. Today we don't use clothes wringers very much. We have drip-dry clothes that can be hung up, and the water just drips out of them without any squeezing or wringing at all. Well, boys and girls, the Bible tells us that we ought to be something like a drip-dry shirt when we give our tithes and offerings to God.

First, God gives us so many blessings we can simply soak them up. But then He wants us to give some of our gifts back to Him. Sometimes, though, we don't want to give them up so easily. We want to keep them for ourselves. The people that lived at the time of the prophet Malachi didn't bring their gifts and God said, " . . . you are robbing me; the whole nation of you. Bring the full tithes into the storehouse, that there may be food in my house, and thereby put me to the test, says the Lord of hosts, if I will not open the windows of heaven for you and pour down for you an overflowing blessing" (Mal. 3:9, 10).

The apostle Paul once asked the Christians in the church of Corinth to gather a gift for the church in Jerusalem. Paul said he wanted the church to give freely. He didn't want to squeeze or wring the gift money out of them.

God wants us to give our gifts with willing and generous hearts. When you give your gift this morning, do you feel like God is squeezing some money out of you the way I squeeze this wash cloth? Or do you really want to give your gifts to Him? Do you feel happy and eager to bring your gift with a loving heart? God wants us to be cheerful givers.

32 Omnipotence

Object: A set of weights

Concept: God is almighty.

Text: *Revelation 19:6* "Hallelujah! For the Lord God omnipotent reigneth!" (KJV)

Boys and girls, these weights are supposed to make you strong. They have a round pipe that is easy to hold *(grasp the rod in the middle and hold it up for all to see).* You can make it as heavy or as light as you want to. The secret is to start with the light ones. *(Add one small weight to either end.)* Then you lift them up like this. *(Do so.)* But you can't do that just once and expect to get strong. No, once doesn't help. You have to lift them up a number of times each day. Then, when you think your muscles are getting stronger, you add a little more weight to each end *(point at additional weights).* So gradually you get stronger and stronger.

Strength or power is really a wonderful thing. Just think of some of the really powerful things that you know about. A huge crane can lift a steel beam weighing many tons from the ground to the roof of a high building as easy as I can lay a book on the table. A locomotive can pull a long train of freight cars. Dynamite can blast solid rock to pieces. The wind is strong enough to move a large sailboat. During a tornado the wind can even blow a building down. Water has power to wash away even huge rocks and trees at a time of a flood.

There are other kinds of strength too, like the strength to stand tall during trouble or sorrow and the strength to resist temptation.

But all the power of man and machine and nature is just a tiny reflection of God's great power. The Bible tells us that God is omnipotent, that is, He is all-powerful, almighty.

The Apostles' Creed says, "I believe in God the Father Almighty, maker of heaven and earth."

How wonderful it is to have a God who is almighty. He can do all things. He puts His loving and powerful arms around us to care for us and keep us. How terrible it would be to have this powerful God as an enemy instead of a friend.

Boys and girls, when you feel your muscles growing stronger, or when you see a powerful machine, or hear a strong wind, remember how strong and how great God is and thank Him for being your God.

33 Omnipresence

Object: Small portable radio

Concept: God is present everywhere.

Text: *II Kings 6:16* "He said, 'Fear not, for those who are with us are more than those who are with them.'"

When I turn my radio on like this *(tune radio in to music so all can hear)* you get music right out of the air, don't you, boys and girls? And if I turn the tuning knob a little, I can get voices of several different people from different radio stations. Most of these stations are quite a long way from here.

But just take a look around at the air *(hold your hands, palms up, and swing them around in the air a bit)*. Now where do you suppose the voices from _____ *(use the call letters of the station or the name of city where the radio station you heard is located)* or the music from _____ are? You can't see the radio waves and you can't hear them without a radio. Television waves are like that too. They're all around you but you can't see them unless you have a television set.

In the Bible there is a story that shows that things we can't see are often very important. The army of the Syrians came to attack the city of Samaria while the prophet Elisha was in the city. Elisha's servant was afraid and he cried out, "Alas, my master, What shall we do?" Then

Elisha said, "Fear not, for those who are with us are more than those that are with them."

Then Elisha prayed that God would open his servant's eyes and suddenly the servant could see the angels that were all around Elisha to guard him and keep him from harm.

Psalm 34:7 tells us that God's angels are all around us, too. It says, "The angel of the Lord encamps around those who fear him, and delivers them."

God protects us by night and by day. He is omnipresent, that is, He is always near us. You can't see Him, can you? But you can't see the radio waves or the television waves either. Still, you know they are there because the minute you turn on the radio or T V you get a program. *(Turn on the radio momentarily and shut it off again.)* Just because you can't see God or His angels doesn't mean they're not there—just turn on the switch of faith and you'll know they're always with you.

34 Omniscience

Object: Your eyes, a stuffed owl, or picture of an owl
Concept: God is an all-seeing God.
Text: *Proverbs 15:3* "The eyes of the Lord are in every place, keeping watch on the evil and the good."

This morning I would like to have you notice my eyes *(point to your eyes)*. I can look straight ahead like this, and I can look at this side of the church *(point and move your eyes to the left)* and to the other side *(now point and move your eyes to the right side)*. My eyes can move from side to side and even up and down, depending on what I would like to see.

But some living things have different kinds of eyes. An owl *(show a stuffed one or a picture if you have it)* can only look straight ahead. If he wants to see something on one side or the other, he has to turn his whole head around. He turns it from side to side. He looks very wise, but that is only because his eyes don't move inside of his head.

If you have a fish in a fishbowl at home, look at his eyes. You'll soon find that he doesn't blink. He doesn't have any eyelids, and never closes his eyes at all.

Flies have such good eyes that they can see almost every direction at once. Maybe you know some other interesting things about animals' eyes, like the way that cats or birds can see. God created our eyes, and all the animals' eyes. But we know from the Bible that God Himself sees us all the time and knows all things. We call this God's omniscience.

It doesn't matter if it is dark or light, if we are near or far away— God can always see us. Sometimes we are glad about this. When we are alone in the dark we are happy to know that God can see us and that He cares for us. But sometimes, if we are doing something we shouldn't be doing, we wish He couldn't see us. But He sees us anyway. The Bible says in Proverbs 15:3, "The eyes of the Lord are in every place, keeping watch on the evil and on the good."

God gave us eyes to see. They remind us that God always sees us too. So, let us always do things that please Him.

35 Pardon

Object: A small chalkboard, eraser, and chalk

Concept: God forgives and forgets our sins.

Text: *Isaiah 55:7* "Let the wicked forsake his way, and the unrighteous man his thoughts; let him return to the Lord, that he may have mercy on him, and to our God, for he will abundantly pardon."

I'm pretty sure that every classroom in school has a chalkboard. I know your teacher likes to use one because it is so easy to clean after the lesson is finished. She writes some questions on the board, and then when you've answered them, she can wipe it clean. Then she can use the chalkboard for another lesson.

Look, I'm going to write on this little chalkboard. Let's put the word *book* on it. *(Write the word in large letters.)* Now I would like one of you boys and girls to come here and erase the word. *(A volunteer cleans the board.)* See what happens? The chalkboard is clean and very soon we forget what word was on it. We can't see it anymore.

Let's try that once again. This time let's write the word *sin. (Write the word.)* Now let's erase it. *(Allow one of the children to do so.)* And once again the chalkboard is clean.

Something like this also happens when God pardons us from our sins. We often hear the word *pardon* when we read about judges and courts in the newspapers, because it is possible for a judge to pardon a person who has committed a crime.

Because we are sinners and do bad things, God is very displeased with us. He doesn't like the bad things that we do. He can punish us like our parents do when we aren't good. But if we love Jesus, then God washes our hearts clean like this chalkboard. When we say, "I'm sorry," and ask God to forgive our sins in Jesus' name, then He pardons us and forgets all those bad things that we have done. He will never punish us for doing them. God washes our hearts clean. He erases the sin. Isn't that wonderful?

Let's try to keep our lives as clean from sin as a chalkboard that's just been cleaned. If we do sin, remember that God wipes our hearts clean when we say to Him, "I'm sorry, God." That's how much God loves us. He washes our hearts clean with the blood of Jesus. He pardons our sins.

36 Patience

Object: Some apple seeds
Concept: We learn patience through much practice in being patient.
Text: *Romans 5:3, 4* "... but we glory in tribulations also: knowing that tribulation worketh patience; and patience, experience; and experience, hope. . . ." (KJV)

Would any of you children like an apple tree in your back yard so you could pick some big red apples? *(Solicit responses—then when a child raises his hand, call him to the front.)* Here are some apple seeds. If you plant these and care for them, you will someday have your apple tree. Just think of the big juicy apples that will grow on it for you. You will be able to climb up on the branches too. So you will have to plant these seeds carefully and someday you'll have an apple tree.

How long do you think it will take for the seed to sprout? *(Wait for child's response.)* That's quite a long time isn't it? And then how long do you think it will be before it grows up big enough to produce its first apple? *(Again wait for the child's response.)* Yes, that will take many years; but someday that time will come. Now you may go back to your seat.

Boys and girls, it's hard to wait, isn't it? If something exciting like a picnic or a trip to the lake is going to happen next week, it seems like time goes so slowly!

Yes, it's hard to be patient. But the Bible tells us that Christians should be patient. We must be patient with one another. We know that we are happy when others are patient with us.

Think of all the people of the Old Testament who looked forward to the time Jesus would be born in Bethlehem. There was Abraham and Isaac and Jacob and David and Isaiah and thousands of others. They all waited for the Savior to come. Now we live after Jesus lived on earth but we must wait too, looking for Him to come back again.

If we get impatient, we must remember that Jesus wants everyone to know about salvation first—everyone in every country in the world. So while we wait for Him to return, we must be busy telling the good news of salvation. Just like _(name)_ , while waiting for his tree to grow apples, will have to take care of the sprout and water the little tree. As it grows, he will have to be very, very patient.

Sometimes when God knows we need to learn how to be more patient, He allows troubles and sickness to come to us. If you get the mumps or measles, you just have to be patient and wait until your sickness is gone before you can go out and play again. So every time we're patient about something, we learn more about how to be patient.

37 Providence

Object: A string of pearls
Concept: God's providence controls all things that happen to us—the things we dislike as well as the things we like.
Text: *Genesis 50:20* "You meant evil against me; but God meant it for good. . . ."

(Begin with your hands cupped together in front of you with a string of pearls inside of them.) I have something in my hands that many people like very much. *(Open your hands and display them.)* It is a string of pearls. Your mother and your sisters have necklaces like these, and someday you girls may wear some of your own. You little boys may be the ones who buy them.

Do you know where pearls come from? They grow inside the shell of an oyster down in the water of the bay.

Not all oysters have pearls in them. A pearl starts to grow when a tiny speck of sand or something else that bothers the oyster gets inside of his shell. Then the oyster's body makes a liquid that goes around the bothersome object and hardens it into a nice shiny pearl.

Oysters that don't have bothersome specks of sand never produce pearls. So men who sell pearls will take a happy oyster and, with a needle, inject an irritating speck inside of the shell and toss the oyster back into the water. A long time later, they open the oyster up and find that he has made a nice shiny pearl—all because of the bothersome thing that got inside of his shell.

Boys and girls, you know that God controls the whole world. He controls our lives too. We call God's care for us His providence. Let's all say that word together so we won't forget it. *(Signal with your hands to encourage the children to say it with you.)* "God's Providence." Remember, God's providence means that nothing can happen to us unless God wants it to happen.

We know that sometimes He sends us many happy blessings. But sometimes He allows troubles to come into our lives. When He allows sickness or sorrow, He is like the oysterman putting something troublesome inside of an oyster's shell.

The troubles and trials make us pray more. They make us think more about how we need God all the time. That's just like the oyster making a pearl, for our prayers and nearness to God are precious both to God and to us.

Joseph's brothers sold him into Egypt, but later when he saw his brothers again he said, "You meant evil against me; but God meant it for good."

When trouble comes into your life, think of the oyster and cover the trouble with prayer and make the trouble into a beautiful pearl of joy and closeness to God.

38 Reconciliation

Object: Two 8" x 10" cards with the numbers 1, 9, 2, 8 on one and the numbers 1, 2, 3, 4 on the other. On the reverse side of both cards place the numbers 1, 2, 3, 4.

Concept: When we are saved, we are once again willing to follow the Lord's leading.

Text: *Ephesians 2:16* "[That Christ] might reconcile us both to God in one body through the cross, thereby bringing the hostility to an end."

Boys and girls, take a long look at these two cards. *(Hold both high but close together.)* Are the numbers on the cards the same? *(Allow the children to respond.)* Of course not! On this card I've got 1, 9, 2, 8 and on this one I have 1, 2, 3, 4. *(Raise card as you read numbers from it.)* These aren't the same numbers. They aren't even in the same order.

Sometimes we are like the mixed-up numbers. God tells us that we should listen to Him. We must obey Him. But we say, "No, God! I want to live my life this way." We're like the numbers that are all out of order. *(Hold up the card with 1, 9, 2, 8.)* We don't want to do what God says.

Do you remember the apostle Paul? He was like this card too. He did many bad things before he loved Jesus. He hurt the people who loved God. God wanted him to be good. God wanted Paul to work for Him, but Paul said, "No." One day, Paul was traveling toward a town. He wanted to hurt the Christians in that town. God sent a very bright light, so bright that Paul fell on the ground and covered his face. But the light blinded him. God was trying to teach him a lesson and was trying to make Paul see that he should obey God. After this happened Paul started obeying God. He became a great missionary.

Sometimes we are like Paul. We don't love God. We are all mixed up like these numbers (hold up the card with 1, 9, 2, 8). We don't want to obey God (hold up the card with numbers 1, 2, 3, 4). But when we love Jesus and say, "I'm sorry, Jesus. Now I want to do what you want me to do," we are reconciled to Jesus. That means that we put our life in order. We want to follow the instructions that God gives us.

Look at these two cards. (Reverse the two cards so that the matched sets appear.) These numbers are the same, aren't they. They agree. They are reconciled. When we see how God wants us to live but don't obey, we are mixed up like the first card. When Jesus saves us we become like these other numbers that are all in order. (Show the 1, 2, 3, 4 cards.) God is pleased when we listen to Him and obey Him.

39 Redemption

Object: A spool of red thread, a red item of clothing, a Bible
Concept: The thread of redemption runs through the Bible from Genesis to Revelation.
Text: *Genesis 3:15* "I will put enmity between you and the woman, and between your seed and her seed; he shall bruise your head, and you shall bruise his heel."

Revelation 5:9 "And they sang a new song, saying, 'Worthy art thou to take the scroll and to open its seals, for thou wast slain and by thy blood didst ransom men for God from every tribe and tongue and people and nation.' "

Boys and girls, have you ever dropped a spool of thread? Did you wind up the thread that got unwound? It seems like there's a long, long thread on one little spool. Just look at this spool of red thread I have in my hand. *(Hold up the spool of thread.)* Do you think the thread on this little spool is long enough to reach way to the back of the room? Let's see if it is. Who will help me? *(Select one child to take one end of the thread and walk to the back of the room while you hold the spool on a thin pencil so it can unwind.)* See how much we've taken off and you can hardly see that anything is gone from the spool. Thank you _____. Now I'll just pull the thread back up here and rewind it later. *(Do so and lay it aside.)* Now look at this red jacket *(or other item of red clothing).* If your mother sews a red jacket like this, she needs thread to hold the buttons on. She needs thread to hold the sleeves and pockets on, too. In fact, she needs thread to hold all the different parts of the jacket together. The thread makes all the separate pieces of cloth hold together so they can be a finished and complete article of clothing.

(Hold up the Bible.) You know the Bible has sixty-six books; it has an Old and a New Testament; it has books of prophecy and books of the gospel and books of epistles. Do you know what holds all the books of the Bible together?

It's the story of redemption—the story of God's plan of salvation. It begins in Genesis where we read about how God made the world and how man sinned. But in Genesis we also find the first promise that Jesus would come to redeem us. And so the story of redemption goes like a red thread through all the books of the Bible to the last chapter of Revelation, where Jesus promises to return.

The Bible tells us something about the history of the children of Israel; it tells us something about science and the world in which we live, but the main purpose of the Bible is to tell us how we can be saved. It tells us how Jesus came to redeem us, that is, how He paid for our sins on the cross. He took our place so that we can have eternal life.

When you see a red jacket, imagine what would happen if no thread held it together—each part would fall off! When you read the Bible remember the thread that holds it all together. Don't miss the big message—the message of redemption through Jesus our Savior.

40 Regeneration

Object: A very dirty drinking glass, a bowl of soapy water, and a dish towel

Concept: God makes us completely new people in Jesus Christ.

Text: *II Corinthians 5:17* "Therefore, if any one is in Christ, he is a new creation; the old has passed away, behold, the new has come."

Boys and girls, do you like to play with very old toys? What about toys that have some pieces missing? *(Allow time for some answers.)* I'm sure that we would all like to have brand new toys. They work so much better and they look so nice.

This drinking glass that I am holding doesn't look very nice *(hold it up with a look of disgust)*. Oh, how dirty it is! It isn't fit to use anymore. Our drinking glasses ought to be clean or else we could get sick. Dirty glasses have germs on them and these germs are bad for us. A glass like this one must be cleaned very well before it is of any use. Let's dip it in this soapy water, and scrub it *(do so)*. Now let's polish it dry with the towel *(do so)*. Look! The drinking glass is clean. It looks almost like a new glass. It is so clean that we can now use it for drinking.

We call this regeneration. Regeneration means to make new again.

We are very much like this glass. When we sin and don't listen to God, we aren't worth very much. God can't use us, just like we couldn't use the dirty glass. But the Bible says that God loves us so much that He cleans us up and makes us over. He regenerates us and makes us into new Christians.

When you help your mother wash dishes, you will see dirty plates. After you wash them carefully, they sparkle and look new. If you fix one of your toys so that it works well again, it will be as good as new. That's just what God does when He regenerates you. He takes away your old sinful self and gives you a new heart that loves God. This is what the apostle Paul says in II Corinthians 5:17: "If anyone is in Christ, he is a new creation, the old has passed away, behold, the new has come." And now we must live like the regenerated boys and girls that God has made us to be.

41 Resurrection

Object: A hand puppet

Concept: After death we will live again.

Text: *I Corinthians 15:52* "For the trumpet shall sound, and the dead will be raised imperishable, and we shall be changed."

I'm sure you all love puppets. I have one here, and his name is Charley. Wave to the boys and girls, Charley. *(Have the puppet make several waving motions to the children.)* He's sort of cute, isn't he? We see puppets like Charley on television. They come in all shapes and sizes.

But all puppets need to have a hand inside. They aren't alive. We pretend that they are but people make the puppet's movements for him. Say, Charley, wave again to the boys and the girls *(again have the puppet wave).*

Now I'm going to take my hand out of the puppet. Look at what happens. Charley is all floppy. *(Hold the puppet by its bottom.)* He can't move anymore. Even though Charley really never was alive, he looks dead now.

When we die, we aren't alive. We can't move, just like Charley here. But the Bible says that we will be alive again. That will be the resurrection. We will be changed, because God will give us life again. That's just like putting my hand back into Charley. Suddenly he can move again. *(Cause the puppet to make several motions.)*

Do you remember the story about Lazarus? Lazarus' two sisters loved him very much. One day he became very sick, and then he died. His friends and his sisters were very sad as they put Lazarus in the grave.

Jesus was Lazarus' friend. When He heard about the death of Lazarus, Jesus also was sad. He went to the grave of His friend. Jesus called to Lazarus with a loud voice, "Lazarus. Come out!" And suddenly, Lazarus became alive again. He was resurrected from the dead. Jesus had the power to raise Lazarus from the dead because He is God.

One day we too will die, but the Bible tells us we will be alive again after our death. So will our grandfathers and grandmothers. Jesus will give us life. This will be our resurrection.

Now let's pretend Charley is alive again. *(Place hand in puppet.)* Wave good-bye, Charley. Remember, boys and girls, when you see a puppet like Charley, think about that fact that we will live again after we die. God will give us this new life.

42 Revelation

Object: A mystery book

Concept: The Bible is God's revelation of Himself; it reveals what God is like and reveals to us His plan of salvation.

Text: *Psalm 119:129-30* "Thy testimonies are wonderful; therefore my soul keeps them. The unfolding of thy words gives light. . . ."

Boys and girls, do you like it when your mother or daddy reads a book to you? You can climb on their laps or sit close by them and listen to a good story. And if you can read for yourself you know that books are good company even when no one else is around. Books can take you to far away places and exciting times.

I have a good book here *(hold it up and add, "from our church library" if your church has one).* It's a mystery story. Did you ever get started on a mystery story and then find it hard to stop in order to study or do your work or even go to bed? Sometimes a teacher may read a really good book to her class. If she's in an especially interesting place when the reading time is over, the class may beg her to go just a little farther so they can find out what will happen next.

Sometimes when you are reading a story, you may wonder how it will end. Then when you do get finished and the whole mystery is solved, you are surprised that you didn't figure it out before. Sometimes you might even peek at the back of the book *(act like you are peeking at the back of the book you are holding)* before you really get that far because you can't wait to find out how the story will turn out.

Yes, books are good friends, and the best book of all is the Bible. The Bible tells us about God. It reveals God to us. There is no other way that we could really know about Him. People in faraway lands who don't have the Bible wonder about God. They imagine what God is like and make all kinds of images of Him. In that way, the Bible is like a mystery book. The Bible solves the mystery of what God is like.

As we begin the story in Genesis we learn a little about God. We learn how He created the whole world and everything that is in it. In Exodus we learn about God's law, the ten commandments. As we read through this wonderful book, we learn more and more about what God is like and God's amazing plan of salvation. Psalm 119:130 says, "The unfolding of thy words gives light. . . ."

When I read my mystery book *(hold up your book again and page through it)* I can hardly wait to see how it will end. But when I get finished reading it, the whole story is ended. The Bible has a wonderful ending part too. It's the book of Revelation. It tells me something about heaven—about the beauty and the joy and the gladness and the praise that will never, never end.

43 Sabbath

Object: A sleeping bag
Concept: Rest is a very important thing for a Christian.
Text: *Exodus 20:8* "Remember the sabbath day, to keep it holy."

Boys and girls, did you know that there was a lady in Africa who didn't sleep for 11 days and 18 hours and 55 minutes? That's a long time to stay awake. That would be like staying awake until _____ *(calculate this length of time: Example, next Wednesday at midnight).*

I'm sure that sometimes you aren't very happy when your mother or father tells you to go to bed. Everything is so much fun that you just don't want to sleep. When you sleep, however, your body rests. It gets ready for another day.

We all sleep best in our beds where it's so nice and warm. But how many of you have ever slept in a sleeping bag like this one? *(Hold up the bag and unzip the side to show the interior.)* A sleeping bag may not be as comfortable as a bed at home, but when we camp in the mountains we can't take our beds along. We can, however, carry sleeping bags and sleep in them. The bags will keep us warm. After hiking all day long in the mountains we need to rest. We unroll the sleeping bag, climb in, and go to sleep.

God gave us time to sleep. That's why we have night. We need to rest. But God also gave us Sunday so that we could rest from everything that we did during the week. Sunday is the sabbath day. Sabbath means rest.

But Sunday isn't a day that we spend in our beds or sleeping bags. Sunday is a day in which we rest up from school. We don't play all of the games or do all the work that we do at school. And when we rest on Sunday we have time to think about God. That's what God wants us to do. That's why He gave us the sabbath. It's a day of rest and a time to think about Him. So, we shouldn't play or work like we do every other day of the week.

God wants us to rest in our beds at night. We need lots of sleep. That lady from Africa needed her sleep. But God wants us to rest on Sunday too. He wants us to think about Him because it is His day. It is a time to stop doing what we always do. Sunday is a time to go to church and to Sunday school.

When we go to bed, we sleep. When you go to bed tonight, remember that God wants you to rest. He wants you to also rest on Sunday and go to church. And when we go to God's house we know we are obeying Him. We will feel ready to go to school again. That's just like we feel when we get out of bed in the morning. We are rested and ready to work. So let's remember that today is Sunday, the day of rest.

44 Sacrament

Object: A light that will make your shadow show on a nearby wall
Concept: Sacraments are like shadows. They remind us that God is real even though we can't see Him.
Text: *I Corinthians 11:24* ". . . Do this in remembrance of me."

Have you ever played shadow tag, boys and girls? Instead of touching someone to catch him and make him "it," you have to step on his shadow.

Shadows are interesting to watch. In the morning when the sun is just coming up, the shadows are long and point toward the west. As the sun goes overhead at noon, the shadows grow shorter. If the sun is exactly above you, you don't have a shadow at all. Then as the sun begins to go down again, the shadows grow longer and point toward the east.

If you study the shape of a shadow, you can tell what it's the shadow of. For example, if you look at the shadow of a tree, you tell if the tree is big and round or thin and tall. If you see the shadow of a dog, you know that a dog is nearby. You can tell what a thing is from its shadow. Look at my shadow on the wall. *(Have the light arranged so the audience can see your shadow on the wall but cannot see you.)* Can you tell that it's me? At least you can tell that a person is nearby. Now if I turn the light off *(do so)* my shadow is gone. If I stayed over here where you couldn't see me, you would think I was gone too. But if I turn the light on again *(do so)* you can see my shadow on the wall. So you know I'm here even though you can't see me. If I turn the light off *(do so again)* and left it off a long, long time, you would probably forget about me. *(Come out of the hiding place to continue the lesson.)*

When Jesus left the earth and went to heaven, He knew that we might forget Him if we didn't see Him. So He left us a sacrament, a reminder, to help us remember what He was like. The night before He died on the cross, Jesus met with His disciples. He took some bread and broke it in pieces, to show how His body would be broken on the cross for us. He took some wine to show how His blood would be shed for our sins. He gave some bread and wine to His disciples to eat and to drink. He said to them and to us, "Do this in remembrance of me." That's why we celebrate the sacrament of the Lord's Supper. All the regular church members take part and I hope all of you boys and girls will too when you grow up. When we see the bread and the wine, we are reminded that Jesus died for our sins. The sacrament is like a shadow. It reminds us that Jesus is really here with us even though we can't see Him.

So the next time you see your shadow, notice how it follows you everywhere you go. Your shadow can help to remind you that Jesus is always with you too.

45 Sacrifice

Object: A winter coat (best used during the winter season)
Concept: The Lord Jesus gave His life so that we might live.
Text: *John 15:13* "Greater love has no man than this, that a man lay down his life for his friends."

Outside it's cold because it's that time of year. We're supposed to have cold weather during the winter. Did you know that the coldest spot in the world is Antarctica? The temperature there once fell to -127°! That's cold!

When the weather gets colder, we have to wear warmer clothes. While we're outside in the cold, clothes help us to stay warm. At night we must use heavier blankets so that we can sleep warmly. Of course during the summer none of these things are necessary, but they are now.

Look at this coat. Let me put it on *(do so)*. Let's pretend that I'm outside in the cold *(make the motions of shivering and rub your hands together)*. Brrrr! But at least with this coat I can stay warm.

But now let's say that I see_____ *(call one of the children forward)*. He's outside in the cold, but he doesn't have a coat. He's very cold. I need this coat to stay warm, but now I see that he needs one too. What am I going to do? What do you think I should do? *(Let the children have a minute to answer.)*

Even though the coat is mine, and I need it to stay warm, I take it off and give it to him. *(Take off the coat and wrap it around the child.)* I have every right to keep this coat, but I give it away.

Jesus did something like that. The Bible says that He loved us so much that He left His home in Heaven to come to earth. He gave up what was His. But even more important, He was willing to give up His life for us. He sacrificed it so that we might have eternal life.

Jesus had every right to stay in Heaven. He had every reason to protect His life, but He gave it all away so that we could become part of God's family. That is a bigger sacrifice than when I gave my coat to_____ *(name the child again).*

Often we don't like to give something that is ours to someone who doesn't have anything. "It's mine!" we say. Remember that Jesus sacrificed His life for us. Let's try to be more like Jesus and be more willing to share and to sacrifice and to give up some of our things to make others happy.

46 Sanctification

Objects: Three shirts or blouses; one dirty and unwashed, one washed but unironed, one washed and ironed neatly

Concept: Sanctification is the process of Christian growth that takes the "wrinkles" or imperfections out of our lives.

Text: *Ephesians 5:26, 27* "... that he might sanctify her, having cleansed her by the washing of water with the word, that he might present the church to himself in splendor, without spot or wrinkle or any such thing, that she might be holy and without blemish."

Have you ever made mud pies? It's lots of fun, isn't it? You just dig in and mix the water and the dirt and squeeze the mud through your fingers. How nice that feels! But sometimes as you play you might wipe your hands on your shirt or blouse and soon it will get very dirty.

What will happen to your shirt or blouse? It will look like this *(hold up dirty shirt)*. It will be quite useless. Your mother would have to throw it away except for one thing—she can wash it. When she does, it will look like this *(hold up washed but wrinkled shirt)*. It has been cleaned but it's not quite ready to wear. It's still all full of wrinkles.

You know how your mother gets the wrinkles out, don't you? She uses a hot iron and presses the wrinkles smooth. Sometimes she has to press a spot more than once before the wrinkles come out. Finally, the shirt or blouse is all ready to wear again.

Do you know what these shirts remind me of? They remind me of people. God made the human race perfect and good, but when Adam and Eve sinned, they became like this shirt—all dirty and useless *(hold up dirty shirt again)*. Then when Jesus washed our sins away, we became all clean like this shirt *(hold up unironed shirt)*. The Bible tells us that He has washed us "whiter than snow." That means He takes all the dirt of our sins away.

But even though Jesus washes our sins away, we still have lots of wrinkles and imperfections in us. So, just like your mother irons the wrinkles out of the shirt and presses it smooth, God uses all the experiences of life, all the things that happen to you, to make you more mature and perfect Christians. Sometimes God uses sickness. Sometimes He uses sorrows and troubles. All these things make us live closer to Him and love Him more. When Christians grow in faith and thankfulness and learn to live better lives, we say they are being *sanctified*. That's what we have to do every day, boys and girls, we have to let God take the wrinkles out, and sanctify us. The Bible tells us that someday Jesus will present the church to Himself as "a glorious church, not having spot or wrinkle or any such thing" (Eph. 5:27). Someday all the wrinkles will be out—that's good news! Jesus has washed our sins away and made us clean *(hold up the clean but wrinkled shirt)*. Every day we have to let God make our lives smooth *(hold up the ironed shirt)*, the way God wants us to be.

47 Temptation

Object: A mouse trap and some cheese
Concept: Satan uses attractive bait to tempt us to sin.
Text: *Matthew 6:13* "And bring us not into temptation, but deliver us from the evil one. . ." (ASV).

If you were a mouse, a very hungry mouse, you would be busy looking for some food to eat. Your nose would help you find what you were looking for. If you were living in my house, and if I had some of this *(hold up cheese)* in my cupboard, you would probably stop and wrinkle your nose and think, "I smell something good to eat." Your nose would tell you where the smell was coming from so you could run over and have a good cheese dinner.

But if I found that a mouse had been eating the cheese in my cupboard, do you know what I would do? I would get a trap like this one *(hold up the trap and snap it)* and set it to try to catch the mouse. But I would have to put some bait on the trap if I wanted to catch anything. Since mice like cheese, I would use cheese on my mousetrap for bait.

Trappers who try to catch coyotes need to use bait that coyotes like. If you want to catch a weasel or a wolf, you have to use some bait that these animals like. A wise trapper knows he has to use the right kind of trap, too. You can't catch a mouse in a bear trap and you can't catch a bear in a mousetrap. Setting the trap in the right place so that the animal will not notice it is also important if you are to catch him.

The devil is something like a wise old trapper. He tries to catch us and make us sin. He uses just the right kind of bait. For some people he uses money, for some he uses fame, for some he uses clothes. And Satan knows just where to set the trap too. He may set a trap for some boy or girl on the playground or on the way home from school to make someone say bad words. He may set a trap on Sunday morning and bait it with sleepiness or on Sunday evening and bait it with a good TV program and he may catch you and keep you from going to church.

When we pray the Lord's prayer we say, ". . . and bring us not into temptation, but deliver us from the evil one. . . ." God can give us the wisdom and the desire to stay out of Satan's traps. If an animal smells a trap on the trail, he will make a wide circle around that spot. He will be very careful to keep out of the trap. We need to be very careful every time Satan tempts us or we too will get caught, just like a mouse in a trap. *(Hold up the trap and snap it to conclude the lesson.)*

48 Trinity

Object: A hard-boiled egg and a knife

Concept: God is one, and God is three persons.

Text: *Matthew 3:16, 17* "And when Jesus was baptized, . . . he saw
the Spirit of God descending like a dove . . . and lo, a voice from
heaven saying, 'this is my beloved Son, with whom I am well
pleased.' "

I have an egg in my hand. Maybe your mother made you one for
breakfast this morning. Sometimes she boils the egg, and some morn-
ings she breaks the egg into a pan and fries it in some butter. Eggs are
good food. We should eat eggs often.

Tell me how many eggs I am holding in my hand *(allow the children
to respond as you hold the egg up)*. Are you sure that I don't have two
eggs, or even three? No, you're right. I do have only one egg in my
hand. It's one white egg that I boiled for a long time this morning
before church.

Let's cut this egg in half. We must do this very carefully. *(Cut the
egg in half, leaving a smooth edge.)* There. Now we have the egg cut in
half. *(Hold up the egg to show the cross section.)* We see now that the
egg has some different parts. We have this hard part on the outside.
That's the shell. Then we see the white part. Finally in the center we

see the yellow part, the yolk. How many parts do we have then? *(Let the children count.)* The shell, the white, and the yolk.

Every one of the three parts is the egg. If an egg didn't have the shell, it would fall apart. It wouldn't be an egg. And if the egg didn't have the white part, it would be all yellow and that wouldn't be good either. And without a yolk the egg is incomplete. One egg has to have these three parts. But it still is only one egg.

Did you know that our triune God is also made up of three parts? We have God the Father, God the Son, and God the Holy Spirit. God is one, though sometimes we talk as if there were three gods. But how can this be?

We will never understand this exactly, but God's oneness is just a little like this egg. Sometimes we see the shell, sometimes we see the white, and sometimes the yolk. But there's really only one egg. All three are needed to make the egg complete.

There is one God. The Bible tells us that God is one God, a triune God. This is hard to understand because at times we see God the Father in the Bible. Then we read about Jesus as God the Son. We also hear about the Holy Spirit. This is the Trinity. God is one God in three persons.

Some people misunderstand what the Bible teaches about God. They think that there are three gods instead of one. But when you eat breakfast, look at your egg *(hold up the egg so the audience can see its three parts)*. It has three parts but it's still one whole egg. Then remember that our triune God is made up of God the Father, God the Son, and God the Holy Spirit. And all together He is one God—the true God—our God.

49 Unity

Object: A paper chain about four feet long

Concept: There is strength and happiness if we are united and work closely together.

Text: *I Corinthians 12:20, 21* "There are many parts, yet one body. The eye cannot say to the hand, 'I have no need of you,' nor again the head to the feet, 'I have no need of you.'"

A chain like the one that I have in my hand is very easy to make. *(Hold the chain by its end to extend it to its full length.)* With just a little glue, some scissors, and some paper, we could make this chain long enough to reach all the way across this church.

But let's look more closely at this chain. I have just one chain. And yet there are all of these little circles or links *(point out several of the links in the chain).* If this chain were a little longer we could tape one end to one wall and the other end to another wall. We could use the chain for the decoration at a birthday party. It is one chain made from lots of little colorful links.

Now I am going to cut this link in the middle of the chain *(cut one of the center links and let the link fall to the floor).* All of a sudden we have two chains *(hold up both chains).* When the chain was just one chain, it had unity. Every link did its part and held the chain together.

103

But this link *(hold up the one that was cut)* decided that he didn't want to be a part of the chain and so the whole chain was broken.

When we do things together we are like a chain. When we play together and share our toys, then everyone is happy. When we are playing together we have unity.

Let's say that the boys are playing basketball. Five boys form a team. When this team works together, everything goes well and the team will win many basketball games.

But when there is no unity, when the team members don't work together, then problems begin. If one boy wants the basketball all of the time, the unity is broken just like this chain was broken *(hold up the two pieces of chain)*.

The Bible has stories about people who didn't want to work together. The disciples of Jesus had an argument one day. Each one of them wanted to be the greatest. They were supposed to be one team of twelve men working together for Jesus. But Peter wanted the most important job. Matthew wanted the same job *(cut two more links out of the chain for emphasis)*. In fact all of the disciples wanted to be the most important one. They weren't showing unity at all. They were separated and alone.

Jesus wants you and me to work and play together without quarreling. He wants us to help our mothers and fathers so we can have unity at home. Jesus wants His followers to be united like a chain.

When you see a truck pulling a heavy load with a chain, remember that each little link in the chain is holding tightly to the next link. The links are all working together. With a spirit of unity or oneness, our church can be a happy place. It can do much for God's kingdom because it is like a chain with every link doing its part.

50 Worldliness

Object: Copies of the following optical illusions on large poster board:

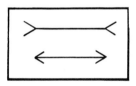 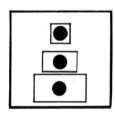

Concept: The things of the world may appear to be more attractive or exciting than the things of God's kingdom, but they really are not.

Text: *I John 2:15* "Do not love the world or the things in the world. . . ."

This morning I have some signs for you to look at. Here is the first one. *(Hold up poster A.)* Look at this one and see if you can tell me which line is longest. If you think the top one is longest, hold up your hand. *(Pause.)* Good! Now all those who think the bottom line is longest, hold up your hand. *(Pause.)* Alright, now all those who think the lines are the same length, hold up your hand. *(Pause.)* Well, we don't quite agree on that one, do we?

Let's try another one. *(Hold up poster B.)* Look at the dots in the squares. How many of you think the top dot is biggest? Hold up your hand. *(Pause.)* Alright, now how many think the bottom circle is biggest? *(Pause.)* How many of you think the dots are all the same size? *(Pause.)* Yes they are. You may come up and measure them after the service if you like. We call these optical illusions.

Boys and girls, the world around us is full of optical illusions. Some things that appear to be important aren't really important at all. Jesus told a parable about a rich man who built many barns to store his grain. He thought that his earthly treasure was the most important thing in the world. But that night he died, and he didn't have any treasure in heaven—which is really the most important kind of treasure.

Many times the things of the world look more attractive and exciting to us than serving God does. But it's only an optical illusion.

The world offers a wide, smooth, and easy way. To many people, the world offers the best road to travel through life, but that's an optical illusion. The road leads to death and destruction. Jesus said that the straight and narrow way is the road that leads to eternal life.

Satan is an expert at optical illusions. He would like to have you choose the things of the world instead of the things of God. But don't be fooled. Check it out and let the Bible tell you what's really true. Serve God instead.